WACKY GOOD CLEAN JOKES

FOR KIDS!

Bob Phillips

HARVEST HOUSE PUBLISHERS
Eugene, Oregon 97402

*Dedicated to the
weird, wild, and wacky
West Family.*

WACKY GOOD CLEAN JOKES FOR KIDS

Copyright © 1995 by Harvest House Publishers
Eugene, Oregon 97402
ISBN 1-56507-458-0

Printed in the United States of America.

96 97 98 99 00 01 02 — 10 9 8 7 6 5 4 3 2 1

Contents

1

Wild Wacky Jokes

Why won't they let wacky people become
  paratroopers?
They can't count to ten.

What do they call a wacky boatload of
  cowards?
Chicken of the Sea.

Why did the wacky boy tiptoe past the
  medicine cabinet?
He didn't want to wake up the sleeping pills.

Why did the wacky girl drive her car off
  the cliff?
She wanted to test her new air brakes.

Why did the wacky man run a steam
  roller over his potato field?
He wanted to raise mashed potatoes.

Why did the wacky family move out of
  their house?
*They heard that more accidents happen at
  home.*

Teacher: Stop acting like a moron.
Wacky boy: I'm not acting.

What do you call a wacky child with half
  a brain?
Gifted.

How many wacky people does it take to
  paint a house?
*1,001—one to hold the brush and 1,000 to
  move the house up and down.*

Why are wacky mothers so strong?
It comes from raising dumbbells.

Why did the wacky girl only buy one
    boot?
*She heard there was a 50-percent chance of
    snow.*

Why did the wacky girl put on a
    blindfold?
So she could go on a blind date.

2

Wendy & Wesley Wacky

Wendy: Why do you call your brother
    Baby Ruth?
Wesley: I have no clue.
Wendy: Because he's half nuts.

Wendy: What do you do when a wacky
    man throws a grenade at you?
Wesley: I can't guess.
Wendy: You pull out the pin and throw it
    back.

Wendy: How much does a wacky man pay
    for a haircut?
Wesley: I have no idea.
Wendy: Four dollars—a buck for each side.

Wendy: What old-West cowboy always
    belches?

Wesley: You tell me.
Wendy: Wyatt Burp.

⚬

Wendy: What do you give a seasick
    elephant?
Wesley: I give up.
Wendy: Plenty of room!

⚬

Wendy: What do you get if you cross a
    germ and a comedian?
Wesley: Who knows?
Wendy: Sick jokes.

⚬

Wendy: Where did Dumbo the Flying
    Elephant land?
Wesley: My mind is a blank.
Wendy: At the earport.

⚬

Wendy: What do you get from an Alaskan
    cow?
Wesley: That's a mystery.
Wendy: Cold cream.

⚬

Wendy: What is red, freezing, and
    dangerous?
Wesley: Tell me.

Wendy: Shark-infested strawberry ice
  cream.

☙❧

Wendy: What do you call a crazy chicken?
Wesley: It's unknown to me.
Wendy: A cuckoo cluck.

☙❧

Wendy: What's the best way to keep milk
  from turning sour?
Wesley: I'm in the dark.
Wendy: Leave it inside the cow.

☙❧

Wendy: What do you get if you cross a
  pile of dirt and a pig?
Wesley: Search me.
Wendy: A groundhog.

☙❧

Wendy: What's a dolphin's favorite TV
  show?
Wesley: You've got me guessing.
Wendy: "Whale of Fortune."

☙❧

Wendy: What has feathers and breaks into
  houses?
Wesley: I'm not sure.
Wendy: A robber ducky.

Wendy: Where does a general keep his armies?
Wesley: How should I know?
Wendy: In his sleevies.

Wendy: What do you get if you cross a road with a 500-pound canary?
Wesley: Give me the answer.
Wendy: Run over.

3
Wacky Knock-Knocks

Knock, knock.
Who's there?
Irish.
Irish who?
Irish you a merry Christmas!

Knock, knock.
Who's there?
Isadore.
Isadore who?
Isadore locked?

Knock, knock.
Who's there?
Omelette.
Omelette who?
Omelette smarter than I look!

Knock, knock.
Who's there?
Hair comb.
Hair comb who?
Hair comb the bride!

Knock, knock.
Who's there?
Censure.
Censure who?
Censure so smart, why aren't you rich?

Knock, knock.
Who's there?
Cain?
Cain who?
Cain you come out to play?

Knock, knock.
Who's there?
Emerson.
Emerson who?
Emerson nice shoes you've got on.

Knock, knock.
Who's there?
Dexter.

Dexter who?
Dexter halls with boughs of holly.

～∞～

Knock, knock.
Who's there?
Gus.
Gus who?
Gus who's coming to dinner?

～∞～

Knock, knock.
Who's there?
Dozen.
Dozen who?
Dozen anybody want to let me in?

～∞～

Knock, knock.
Who's there?
Wayne.
Wayne who?
Wayne drops keep falling on my head.

～∞～

Knock, knock.
Who's there?
Apricot.
Apricot who?
Apricot my key. Open up!

4

Winthrop & Whitney Wacky

Winthrop: What do they call it when a wacky boy washes his hands?
Whitney: I have no clue.
Winthrop: Erosion.

Winthrop: How do you keep an elephant from going through the eye of a needle?
Whitney: I don't know.
Winthrop: Tie a knot in his tail.

Winthrop: What is it called when a man marries the boss' daughter?
Whitney: Beats me.
Winthrop: Fire insurance.

Winthrop: What's the biggest laundry
  problem giraffes have?
Whitney: I can't guess.
Winthrop: Ring around the collar.

Winthrop: What do you get when you
  cross an elephant with a computer.
Whitney: I have no idea.
Winthrop: A 5000-pound know-it-all.

Winthrop: What's at the opposite end of
  "de" animal's head?
Whitney: You tell me.
Winthrop: Detail.

Winthrop: Why did the wacky man always
  handle money with his toes?
Whitney: I give up.
Winthrop: So it wouldn't slip through his
  fingers.

Winthrop: How long can a goose stand on
  one leg?
Whitney: Who knows?
Winthrop: Try it and see.

Winthrop: What sort of offspring does a
　　wacky florist have?
Whitney: You've got me.
Winthrop: Blooming idiots.

∽o∾

Winthrop: What did one bowl of pudding
　　say to the other bowl of pudding?
Whitney: My mind is a blank.
Winthrop: You're pudding me on.

∽o∾

Winthrop: What happens to a lion who
　　crosses the desert on Christmas Day?
Whitney: That's a mystery.
Winthrop: He gets sandy claws.

∽o∾

Winthrop: What do you say when you
　　meet a two-headed monster?
Whitney: Tell me.
Winthrop: "Hello, hello!"

∽o∾

Winthrop: What do they call a collector of
　　old magazines?
Whitney: I don't have the foggiest.
Winthrop: A doctor.

∽o∾

Winthrop: What do we need armies for?

Whitney: It's unknown to me.
Winthrop: To keep our handies on.

❦

Winthrop: Who was Snow White's brother?
Whitney: I'm in the dark.
Winthrop: Egg White . . . get the yolk?

❦

Winthrop: What is the Lone Ranger's first
name?
Whitney: Search me.
Winthrop: The.

❦

Winthrop: What is another name for a
cracked pot?
Whitney: You've got me guessing.
Winthrop: A psycho-ceramic.

❦

Winthrop: What do you call a carpenter
who lends tools to his neighbor?
Whitney: I'm not sure.
Winthrop: A saw loser.

❦

Winthrop: How do you know when
there's an elephant in your bed?
Whitney: How should I know?
Winthrop: By the E on his pajamas.

Winthrop: What is purple and crazy?
Whitney: Give me the answer.
Winthrop: A grape nut.

5

Walloping Wackys

Teacher: All right, let's hear you count to ten.

Wacky student: One, two, three, four, five, six, seven, eight, nine, ten.

Teacher: That's fine. Can you go a little higher?

Wacky student: Jack, Queen, King.

∽∾

Man on the street: Why do you keep standing at the bus stop as the buses go by?

Wacky man: I was told to take the 14th Street bus. But so far only ten have gone by.

∽∾

Wacky woman: It's been two weeks since my last visit and I still don't feel any better.

Doctor: I don't understand it. Did you follow the instructions on the pills I gave you?

Wacky woman: I sure did. It said "Keep this bottle tightly closed."

Wacky husband: Hey! Look at this VCR I got.

Wacky wife: I told you we can't afford one of those.

Wacky husband: It's okay. I traded the TV for it.

Wacky husband: What's today's date?

Wacky wife: Why don't you just look at the newspaper in your hand?

Wacky husband: That's no good—it's yesterday's paper.

Teacher: Name two cities in Iowa.

Wacky student: Okay. I'll name one Floyd and the other one Irving.

6

Wacky Waiters

Customer: Waiter, there's a footprint in
my breakfast!

Wacky waiter: Well, you ordered an
omelet and told me to step on it.

Customer: Waiter! There's no chicken in
my chicken soup!

Wacky waiter: There's no horse in the
horseradish, either.

Customer: Waiter, why is your finger on
my steak?

Wacky waiter: To keep it from falling on
the floor again.

Customer: Waiter! There's a bee in my
soup!

Wacky waiter: Of course, sir. It's alphabet soup.

Customer: Waiter, there's a fly in my soup.
Wacky waiter: Don't worry, sir, the spider on the bread will take care of it.

Customer: There's a frog in my soup!
Wacky waiter: Yes, sir. The fly's on holiday.

Customer: Waiter! There's a fly in my soup!
Wacky waiter: Just a moment, sir—I'll get some fly spray.

Customer: Waiter! There's a fly in my soup!
Wacky waiter: Go ahead and eat him, there's more where he came from.

Customer: Waiter! What's this cockroach doing in my soup?
Wacky waiter: We ran out of flies.

Customer: Waiter! There's a fly in my soup!

Wacky waiter: Just wait until you see the main course.

≈∘≈

Customer: Is your water supply healthy?

Wacky waiter: Yes, sir. We only use well water.

≈∘≈

Customer: Waiter! I'm so hungry I could eat a horse!

Wacky waiter: You certainly came to the right place.

≈∘≈

Customer: Waiter! There's a dead fly swimming in my soup!

Wacky waiter: Nonsense, sir. Dead flies can't swim.

≈∘≈

Customer: Waiter! There's a fly in my applesauce!

Wacky waiter: Of course! It's a fruit fly.

≈∘≈

Customer: What is this cockroach doing on my ice-cream sundae?

Wacky waiter: I think it's skiing.

∽o∾

Customer: Waiter, there's a fly in my bean soup.
Wacky waiter: Don't worry mister. Here, I'll take it back and exchange it for a bean.

∽o∾

Customer: You've brought me the wrong order!
Wacky waiter: Well, you did say you wanted something different.

∽o∾

Customer: Waiter, what is this fly doing in my ice cream?
Wacky waiter: Maybe he likes winter sports.

∽o∾

Customer: Waiter, did you know there is a fly in my soup?
Wacky waiter: That's not a fly, sir, it's just dirt in the shape of a fly.

7

Wilma & Warren Wacky

Wilma: Why won't weathermen tell each
   other jokes?
Warren: I have no clue.
Wilma: They don't want to laugh up a
   storm.

Wilma: Why are the floors of basketball
   courts always so damp?
Warren: I don't know.
Wilma: The players dribble a lot.

Wilma: Who wiggles, hisses, and runs a
   country?
Warren: Beats me.
Wilma: The president of the United Snakes.

Wilma: Who has seven eyes, lives under-
   ground, and conquered the world?

Warren: I can't guess.
Wilma: Alexander the Potato.

∽o∼

Wilma: Who is the funniest goat?
Warren: I have know idea.
Wilma: Billy the Kidder.

∽o∼

Wilma: Who rides on a raft, hates school, and hardly ever eats?
Warren: You tell me.
Wilma: Huckleberry Thin.

∽o∼

Wilma: Which president had big sharp teeth?
Warren: I give up.
Wilma: Jaws Washington.

∽o∼

Wilma: How do you hit slime?
Warren: Who knows?
Wilma: With a sludgehammer.

∽o∼

Wilma: How do loudmouths pay for college?
Warren: You've got me.
Wilma: They get hollerships.

∽o∼

Wilma: How can you make a moth ball?
Warren: My mind is a blank.
Wilma: Hit him with a flyswatter.

Wilma: How do comics like their eggs
    cooked?
Warren: That's a mystery.
Wilma: Funny-side-up.

Wilma: How would you describe a boring,
    ordinary shopping center?
Warren: Tell me.
Wilma: Run-of-the-mall.

Wilma: What is fat, green, and goes
    "Oink, oink"?
Warren: I don't have the foggiest.
Wilma: Porky Pickle.

Wilma: What do you call a person who is
    broke and stranded in the mall?
Warren: It's unknown to me.
Wilma: Shopwrecked.

Wilma: What has antlers and eats cheese?

Warren: I'm in the dark.
Wilma: Mickey Moose.

∽o∾

Wilma: What gives milk, goes "moo, moo," and makes all your dreams come true?
Warren: Search me.
Wilma: Your Dairy Godmother.

∽o∾

Wilma: What is a whale's favorite game?
Warren: You've got me guessing.
Wilma: Swallow the Leader.

∽o∾

Wilma: What famous nurse never had time to get dressed in the morning?
Warren: How should I know?
Wilma: Florence Nightingown.

∽o∾

Wilma: What is a parrot's favorite game?
Warren: Give me the answer.
Wilma: Hide 'n Speak.

∽o∾

Wilma: What was the name of Cinderella's fairy godmother?
Warren: I have no clue.
Wilma: Wanda.

Wilma: What weighs three tons, is gray, and flies?
Warren: I don't know.
Wilma: A hippo on a hang glider.

Wilma: What does a frog order at a fast-food restaurant?
Warren: Beats me.
Wilma: A burger and flies.

8

Witty Wackys

What do wacky people and pop bottles have in common?
They're both empty from the neck up.

How do you get a wacky girl's eyes to sparkle?
Shine a flashlight in her ear.

How do you give a wacky man a brain transplant?
Blow in his ear.

What does a wacky man say after you blow in his ear?
Thanks for the refill.

What does a smart wacky person and a
dinosaur have in common?
Both are extinct.

What is the difference between Bigfoot
and a smart wacky person?
There have been sightings of Bigfoot.

What is a wacky girl doing when she holds
her hands tightly over her ears?
She is trying to hold a thought.

What do you call a school of higher
learning for wacky people?
Any grade school with a second floor.

Why do wacky girls wear big, heavy,
dangling earrings?
So the air won't blow their head away.

Why did the wacky man get fired from
the M & M factory?
He kept throwing out the W's.

9

Did You Hear About the Wackys?

Did you hear the wacky story about the
    little wooden boy named Pinocchio?
No.
He got caught out in a rainstorm and
    ended up with a warped mind.

Did you hear about the wacky national
    lottery?
Not yet.
You can win a dollar a year for a million
    years.

Did you hear the wacky joke about the
    lion?
I don't think so.
When you hear it you will roar.

Did you hear about the wacky fisherman
who chartered a helicopter?
Is it funny?
He wanted to catch flying fish.

～o～

Did you hear the wacky joke about the
garbage dump?
What happened?
You wouldn't like it because it's a lot of
rubbish.

～o～

Did you hear about the wacky dentist who
went into the army?
Tell me.
They made him a drill sergeant.

～o～

Did you hear the wacky joke about the
playing cards?
What about it?
It's no big deal.

～o～

Did you hear about the wacky lady who
spent weeks shopping for a color TV?
No.
She couldn't decide which color to buy.

～o～

Did you hear about the wacky man who
    got stuck in the revolving door?
Not yet.
He doesn't get around much anymore.

Did you hear about the wacky woman
    who got her head stuck in the
    washing machine?
I don't think so.
She ended up brainwashed.

Have you heard the wacky joke about the
    express train?
I don't think so.
You just missed it.

Have you heard about the wacky cow who
    got caught in the earthquake?
Was she hurt?
Don't worry, she gives terrific milkshakes.

Did you hear the wacky joke about the
    sun?
What happened?
I think it's way over your head.

Did you hear about the wacky boy who
went to summer camp for two weeks?
*His mother told him to put on a fresh pair of
socks every day, but he couldn't fit fourteen
pairs over his shoes!*

Did you hear about the wacky college
student who wrote home and told his
mother that he had grown another
foot?
His mother knitted him a third sock.

Did you hear about the wacky athlete who
was really dumb?
*When he earned his varsity letter, someone had
to read it to him.*

10
Winifred & Wilbur Wacky

Winifred: What happens when a flock of
   geese lands in a volcano?
Wilbur: I have no clue.
Winifred: They cook their own gooses.

Winifred: What do you get if you cross a
   steer with a tadpole?
Wilbur: I don't know.
Winifred: A bullfrog.

Winifred: When do kangaroos celebrate
   their birthdays?
Wilbur: Beats me.
Winifred: During leap year.

Winifred: What do they call the friend-
   ship that one wacky actor has for
   another?

Wilbur: I can't guess.
Winifred: Jealousy.

Winifred: What did Snow White say
when her pictures did not arrive back
from the photo service?
Wilbur: I have no idea.
Winifred: Someday my prints will come.

Winifred: If a thief falls into cement, what
does he become?
Wilbur: You tell me.
Winifred: A hardened criminal.

Winifred: What is green and pecks on
trees?
Wilbur: I give up.
Winifred: Woody-Wood Pickle.

Winifred: What do you call a dumb
skeleton?
Wilbur: Who knows?
Winifred: A bone-head.

Winifred: What do they call a fellow who
introduces his best girl to his best
friend?
Wilbur: You've got me.
Winifred: An idiot.

Winifred: What's the best way to tell an
elephant with a short temper that he's
fired?
Wilbur: My mind is a blank.
Winifred: You call him long distance.

Winifred: What is big and hairy, wears a
dress, and climbs up the Empire State
Building?
Wilbur: That's a mystery.
Winifred: Queen Kong.

Winifred: How do you prevent 500-pound
canaries from attacking you on safaris?
Wilbur: Tell me.
Winifred: Use 500-pound canary
repellant.

Winifred: How do we know that owls are
smarter than chickens?
Wilbur: I don't have the foggiest

Winifred: Have you ever heard of
Kentucky Fried owl?

⌘

Winifred: How do you milk a caterpillar?
Wilbur: It's unknown to me.
Winifred: First you find a very low stool. . . .

⌘

Winifred: Where does Robin Hood buy
flowers for Maid Marian?
Wilbur: I'm in the dark.
Winifred: At the Sherwood florist.

⌘

Winifred: How do you fix a broken
tomato?
Wilbur: Search me.
Winifred: With tomato paste.

⌘

Winifred: How did the nervous carpenter
break his teeth?
Wilbur: You've got me guessing.
Winifred: He bit his nails.

⌘

Winifred: If cowboys ride horses, what do
you call someone who rides cows?
Wilbur: I'm not sure.
Winifred: Weird.

Winifred: If your father told dumb jokes,
    what would you call him?
Wilbur: How should I know?
Winifred: Pop-corn.

Winifred: Where do hip geologists go to
    have a good time?
Wilbur: Give me the answer.
Winifred: To rock festivals.

11

Wacky Winners

How do wacky fishermen count their daily
   catch of fish?
*One fish . . . two fish . . . another fish . . . another
fish . . . another fish.*

Why did the wacky big-game hunter give
   up hunting for elephants?
He got tired of carrying the decoys.

Do you know why wacky dogs have flat
   noses?
From chasing parked cars.

How can you tell the difference between a
   wacky person and a gorilla?
The gorilla peels the banana before he eats it.

How do you make a wacky girl laugh on
   Monday?
Tell her a joke on Friday.

Why was the little wacky kid so upset when
   the label fell off his yellow crayon?
He wanted to know what color it was.

What happened to the wacky boy when
   he learned that he had been promoted
   from second grade to third grade?
He was so excited he cut himself while shaving.

Why do wacky people drink less Kool-Aid
   than other folks?
*Because they have such a hard time getting two
   quarts of water into those little envelopes.*

Why does it take two wacky soldiers to
   handle one rifle?
*It takes one to pull the trigger, and one to go
   find the cork and put it back in the gun.*

Why doesn't the machine shop give their
   wacky mechanics a coffee break?
It takes too long to retrain them.

Two wacky men were arguing about some
    tracks they found while hunting:
      "They're lion tracks!"
      "No, they're bear tracks!"
While they were arguing, a train ran over
    them.

Two wacky boys were walking down a
    railroad track. The first one said,
    "These long stairs sure do get me."
"It's not the stairs," responded the second.
    "It's these low banisters."

Wacky wife: Who was that on the phone?
Wacky husband: Just someone who said it
    was long distance from Russia. I said it
    sure was.

A wacky boy swallowed his watch by
    accident. His friend asked, "Does it
    hurt much?"
The wacky boy answered, "Only when I
    wind it."

12

Wacky Definitions

What do they call abalone?
An expression of disbelief.

What do they call an alarm clock?
A mechanical device to wake up people who don't have small children.

What do they call an autobiography?
The life story of an automobile.

What do they call a babysitter?
Someone you pay to watch your television and eat your food.

What do they call a bad driver?
The guy you run into.

What do they call a bank robber?
A guy who gets alarmed easily.

What is a basketball?
A dance held in a basket.

What do they call behold?
*What one bee wrestler uses to pin another bee
    wrestler.*

What is a boss?
*The one who is early when you are late and late
    when you are early.*

What is a cartoon?
A song sung in an automobile.

What do they call a chicken inspector?
A worker who's a cluck watcher.

13
Wimple & William Wacky

Wimple: What is white, lives in the
    Himalayas, and lays eggs?
William: I have no clue.
Wimple: The abominable snow chicken.

Wimple: What's hairy, rules England, and
    loves bananas?
William: I don't know.
Wimple: King Henry the Ape.

Wimple: What do you get when you cross
    a stallion with a possum?
William: Beats me.
Wimple: A horse that hangs by its tail.

Wimple: What do you get when you cross
    a praying mantis and a termite?
William: I can't guess.

Wimple: A bug that says grace before eating your house.

Wimple: What's faster than a speeding bullet, more powerful than a loco-motive, able to leap tall buildings in a single bound, and has a ten-acre parking lot?
William: I have no idea.
Wimple: Supermarket!

Wimple: Where did Abraham Lincoln keep his pigs?
William: You tell me.
Wimple: In a hog cabin.

Wimple: What do you get when you cross a grizzly bear with vanishing cream?
William: I give up.
Wimple: Nobody knows. It's gone before you get a good look.

Wimple: What lives in the ocean, is grouchy, and hates neighbors?
William: Who knows?
Wimple: A hermit crab.

Wimple: What's worse than an elephant
　　on water skis?
William: You've got me.
Wimple: A porcupine in a rubber raft.

Wimple: Where do you find a
　　down-and-out octopus?
William: My mind is a blank.
Wimple: On Squid Row.

Wimple: Why did the unwashed chicken
　　cross the road twice?
William: That's a mystery.
Wimple: Because it was a dirty
　　double-crosser.

Wimple: Why did the cow cross the road?
William: Tell me.
Wimple: Because it was the chicken's day
　　off.

Wimple: Why didn't the elephant cross
　　the road?
William: I don't have the foggiest.
Wimple: He didn't want to be mistaken
　　for a chicken.

Wimple: Why did the pig go to the casino?

William: It's unknown to me.

Wimple: He wanted to play the slop machine.

Wimple: Why do dogs run in circles?

William: I'm in the dark.

Wimple: It's hard to run in squares.

Wimple: Why did the chicken cross the road to the amusement park?

William: Search me.

Wimple: To get to the other ride.

Wimple: How should a jogger wash his sneakers?

William: You've got me guessing.

Wimple: In running water.

Wimple: Why did the whale cross the road?

William: I'm not sure.

Wimple: To get to the other tide.

Wimple: Why do buffalos always travel in
  herds?
William: How should I know?
Wimple: Because they're afraid of getting
  mugged by elephants.

Wimple: Why did the judge send for a
  locksmith?
William: Give me the answer.
Wimple: The key witness was missing.

14
Wacky Wit

Professor to wacky students: *If you get this information in your brain you will have it in a nutshell.*

Wacky mugger: This is a holdup! Give me your money or else.
Victim: Or else what?
Wacky mugger: Don't confuse me. This is my first job.

Did you hear about the wacky athlete that was injured in football practice?
The coach gave him the ball and told him to run around his own end.

Wacky patient: Doctor, how long can a person live without a brain?
Doctor: I give up. How old are you?

First wacky boy: My girlfriend's really
   smart. She has brains enough for two.
Second wacky boy: Sounds like the right
   girl for you.

Did you hear about the wacky water polo
   player?
His horse drowned.

Wacky man: Doctor, I think there are
   grapes growing in my ears.
Doctor: That is impossible!
Wacky man: Thank goodness! I planted
   bananas.

What happened when the wacky boy had
   a brain transplant?
The brain rejected him.

Did you hear about the wacky girl who
   spent four hours trying to figure out a
   jigsaw puzzle?
*She gave up because she couldn't get the two
   pieces to fit together.*

What's the difference between a monkey
    and a wacky person?
You can hold a conversation with a monkey.

What did the wacky man do when he
    heard that 90 percent of all serious
    accidents happen around the home?
He moved.

What happened to the wacky sea scout?
His tent sank.

Did you hear about the wacky teacher
    who increased her students desire to
    learn to read?
*They wanted to know what all of her tattoos
    said.*

15
Worn-Out Wackys

Did you hear about the wacky mother
who bought her son some Silly Putty
to play with?
It outsmarted him.

I know one wacky woman who is so boring
at parties that she stays in the room
with the coats.
Sometimes a few of the coats even leave!

Did you hear about the wacky cook?
He was so bad that he burned the Jell-O!

Did you hear about the wacky boy who
had an invisible friend to play with?
Everyone could see him except the wacky boy.

Did you hear about the wacky family that bought their children educational toys to play with?
They went to college and majored in Slinky.

Did you hear about the wacky athelete who hit a home run?
Unfortunately they were playing football at the time.

Did you hear abut the wacky boy who received a set of bookends for his birthday?
He hasn't had time to read them yet.

Where did they film the movie *Lost in Space*?
In a wacky person's head.

Cowhand: Aren't you putting your saddle on backward, sir?
Wacky man: A lot you know about it! You don't even know which direction I'm going to go.

Sergeant: Does your uniform fit you satisfactorily?

Wacky officer: The shirt is all right. But the pants are a little too tight around the armpits.

Commanding officer: You're not wearing your parachute!
Wacky soldier: It's okay. We're just practicing, aren't we?

Officer (at the shooting range): Get ready. Aim. Fire at will.
Wacky soldier: Which one is Will?

Did you hear about the wacky man who took his dog to obedience school?
The dog passed; he flunked.

Teacher: Robert Burns wrote "To a Field Mouse."
Wacky student: Did the field mouse write back?

Fellow student: Have you ever taken chloroform?
Wacky student: No. Who teaches it?

16
Willard & Walter Wacky

Willard: What were Alexander Graham
Bell's first words?
Walter: I have no clue.
Willard: "Goo-goo."

Willard: What do you get if you dial
1-853-1013-76298-0056834?
Walter: I don't know.
Willard: A sore finger.

Willard: What's the most exact body of
water?
Walter: Beats me.
Willard: The Specific Ocean.

Willard: What legendary character steals
from the rich and keeps it?
Walter: I can't guess.
Willar: Robin Hoodlum.

Willard: Where do cows go on vacation?
Walter: I have no idea.
Willard: Moo York.

Willard: What is the name of the story
about the athlete and the giant?
Walter: You tell me.
Willard: "Jock and the Beanstalk."

Willard: What powerful reptile lives in
Emerald City?
Walter: I give up.
Willard: The Lizard of Oz.

Willard: What does a parrot say on the
Fourth of July?
Walter: Who knows?
Willard: "Polly wants a firecracker!"

Willard: What do you call a boomerang
that doesn't come back?
Walter: You've got me.
Willard: A stick.

Willard: Where does the gingerbread man sleep?
Walter: My mind is a blank.
Willard: Under a cookie sheet.

❧

Willard: What is gray, has short antennae, large wings, a long nose, and gives money to elephants?
Walter: Tell me.
Willard: The tusk fairy.

❧

Willard: What was Samuel Clemens' pen name?
Walter: I don't have the foggiest.
Willard: He never had a name for his pen.

❧

Willard: What kind of bee hums and drops things?
Walter: It's unkown to me.
Willard: A fumble bee.

❧

Willard: Where does seaweed look for a job?
Walter: I'm in the dark.
Willard: In the kelp wanted ads.

❧

Willard: What does a lima bean wear on its head?
Walter: Search me.
Willard: A lima beanie.

Willard: What is large, yellow, has never been photographed, and lives in Scotland?
Walter: You've got me guessing.
Willard: The Lochness canary.

Willard: What did the banana say to the elephant?
Walter: I'm not sure.
Willard: Nothing. Bananas can't talk.

Willard: What should you say when you meet a toad?
Walter: How should I know?
Willard: Wart's new?

Willard: Where do you send old detectives?
Walter: Give me the answer.
Willard: To the clue factory.

17

Wondrous Wackys

City slicker: Boy, you sure have a lot of flies around your horses and cows. Do you ever shoo them?

Wacky rancher: Nope. We just let them go barefoot.

⧜

Did you hear about the wacky boy who went to the amusement park? He decided to try the tunnel of love with his girlfriend. When they came out they were drenched.

"What happened?" asked a friend. "Did the boat leak?"

The wacky couple looked surprised. "What boat?"

⧜

Did you hear about the wacky man who died at the age of 43?

He was nailing a horseshoe over his door and the horse fell on his head.

Then there was the wacky woman who drove up in front of the hospital. She saw the sign that said *Fine for parking*— so she parked!

Then there was the wacky girl who was driving to Los Angeles to visit her brother in the hospital. But when she saw a sign on the freeway that said *Los Angeles Left* she went home.

Why did the wacky girl stand in front of the mirror with her eyes shut?
So she could see what she looked like when she was asleep.

While the wacky girl was showing off her new magnifying glass, her friend said, "I see this magnifies things four times."
"Rats!" cried the girl. "I've used it three times already!"

What is the worst advice you can give to a wacky woman who is going for a job interview?
Be yourself.

What is the best reason to hire a wacky man?
When he goes on vacation, you don't have to hire a replacement to do his work.

What do you call a wacky man with half a brain?
Brilliant.

What is it called when you play a game of wits with a wacky person?
Solitaire.

What happens when a wacky kid takes a sick day from school?
The teacher sends a thank-you note home.

Why don't wacky kids play hide-and-seek?
Who would come looking for them?

18

Walloping Wacky Jokes

Did you hear about the wacky musician
who played piano by ear? She died
last week.

"How come?"

She got her earring caught between the
keys and starved to death.

Did you hear about the wacky terrorist
who tried to blow up a bus?

He burnt his lips on the exhaust pipe.

Did you hear about the wacky man who
went ice fishing?

He brought back 50 pounds of ice.

Did you hear about the wacky schoolboy?

He had to get a tutor so he could pass recess!

19
More Wacky Knock-Knocks

Knock, knock.
Who's there?
Sloane.
Sloane who?
Sloane Ranger rides again.

Knock, knock.
Who's there?
Shelby.
Shelby who?
Shelby coming around the mountain when
    she comes.

Knock, knock.
Who's there?
Police.
Police who?
Police hurry up! It's chilly outside.

Knock, knock.
Who's there?
Sara.
Sara who?
Sara doctor in the house? These
    jokes are sick.

Knock, knock.
Who's there?
Adair.
Adair who?
Adair you to open this door.

Knock, knock.
Who's there?
Clark.
Clark who?
Clark clark, I'm a chicken.

Knock, knock.
Who's there?
Fido.
Fido who?
Fido known you were coming, I would
    have baked a cake.

Knock, knock.
Who's there?
Wooden shoe.
Wooden shoe who?
Wooden shoe like to know?

Knock, knock.
Who's there?
York.
York who?
York, york, york. This is funny.

Knock, knock.
Who's there?
Ben Hur.
Ben Hur who?
Ben Hur an hour and and no one has
    opened the door.

Knock, knock.
Who's there?
Eisenhower.
Eisenhower who?
Eisenhower late for work.

Knock, knock.
Who's there?
Heywood.

Heywood who?
Heywood you please open the door?

Knock, knock.
Who's there?
Turner.
Turner who?
Turner handle and let me in.

20
Wanda & Wilson Wacky

Wanda: What do Alexander the Great and
   Smokey the Bear have in common?
Wilson: I have no clue.
Wanda: They both have the same middle
   name.

Wanda: How much does an idiot weigh?
Wilson: I don't know.
Wanda: Step on the scales and see.

Wanda: Why did the chicken cross the
   road?
Wilson: Beats me.
Wanda: For fowl reasons.

Wanda: Who wears a crown, lives in a
   delicatessen, and calls for his fiddlers
   three?

Wilson: I can't guess.
Wanda: Old King Coleslaw.

∽◦∾

Wanda: Where does a two-ton gorilla sit
when he goes to the movies?
Wilson: I have no idea.
Wanda: Anywhere he wants to!

∽◦∾

Wanda: What is another name for a smart
duck?
Wilson: You tell me.
Wanda: A wise quacker.

∽◦∾

Wanda: What is black and white and red
all over?
Wilson: I give up.
Wanda: A sunburned penguin.

∽◦∾

Wanda: What did the man do when he
heard he was going to die?
Wilson: Who knows?
Wanda: He went into the living room.

∽◦∾

Wanda: Who invented the grandfather
clock?

Wilson: You've got me.
Wanda: Pendulum Franklin.

❦

Wanda: If your letter carrier falls in the mud, what do you get?
Wilson: My mind is a blank.
Wanda: Blackmail.

❦

Wanda: What is big and green and eats rocks.
Wilson: That's a mystery.
Wanda: A big, green rock-eater.

❦

Wanda: How does the Lone Ranger keep his horse so shiny?
Wilson: Tell me.
Wanda: Silver polish.

❦

Wanda: What is a monster's normal eyesight?
Wilson: I don't have the foggiest.
Wanda: 20/20/20/20/20.

❦

Wanda: How does a musician clean his tuba?
Wilson: It's unknown to me.
Wanda: With a tuba toothpaste, naturally!

Wanda: How did Mother Hubbard
    describe her cupboard when she found
    it empty?
Wilson: I'm in the dark.
Wanda: Uncanny.

Wanda: What do you call a trainer who
    sticks his right hand in a lion's
    mouth?
Wilson: Search me.
Wanda: Lefty.

Wanda: What do you get when you pour
    hot water down a rabbit hole?
Wilson: You've got me guessing.
Wanda: A hot cross bunny!

Wanda: Who was King Midas?
Wilson: I'm not sure.
Wanda: He was the Greek king who fixed
    chariot mufflers.

Wanda: When a wacky dairy farmer milks
    his cows, what do you call his jokes?
Wilson: How should I know?
Wanda: Udder nonsense!

Wanda: What's green and goes slam, slam, slam, slam?
Wilson: Give me the answer.
Wanda: A four-door pickle.

21

Well-Worn Wackys

Wacky woman: Oh, Mr. Policeman! Mr. Policeman! A man is following me and I think he's crazy!

Policeman: I agree!

Wacky burglar: The police are coming! Quick, jump out the window!

Wacky accomplice: But we're on the thirteenth floor!

Wacky burglar: This is no time to be superstitious!

First wacky boy: It was sure hard to peddle this bicycle-built-for-two up this mile-long hill.

Second wacky boy: You're right. It was hard, and scary too.

First wacky boy: Scary?

Second wacky boy: Yeah! It was a good
thing I kept the brakes on or we would
have rolled back down the hill.

First wacky boy: What's so unusual about
your girlfriend?
Second wacky boy: She chews on her
nails.
First wacky boy: Lots of girls chew on
their nails.
Second wacky boy: Toenails?

First wacky man: My girlfriend has a
huge lower lip, but I don't mind.
Second wacky man: You don't?
First wacky man: No, her upper lip
covers it!

Husband: This bread is nice and warm!
Wacky wife: It should be . . . the cat's been
sitting on it all day!

First wacky woman: What's that peculiar
odor I smell around this post office?
Second wacky woman: Probably the dead
letters.

First wacky girl: Is it good manners to eat
chicken with your fingers?
Second wacky girl: No, you should eat
your fingers separately.

A wacky girl was walking down the street
with an ugly, miserable-looking turkey
under her arm.
"Where did you get it?" asked a person on
the street corner.
"I won her in a raffle," replied the turkey.

Wacky woman: You see, Doctor, I have
this habit of collecting spaghetti. My
entire living room is filled with it.
Psychiatrist: Why don't you put it in the
closet?
Wacky woman: There's no room—that's
where I keep the meatballs.

Did you hear about the wacky man who
was so stupid that he stayed up all
night studying?
He had a blood test the next morning.

Wacky boy: Ah, look at the cow and the
calf rubbing noses in the pasture. That
sight makes me want to do the same."

Wacky girl: Well, go ahead . . . it's your
　　cow.

∞○∞

Wacky girl: I would like two tickets for the
　　movie.
Ticket seller: I am sorry, but we only have
　　standing room.
Wacky girl: Do you have two together?

22

More "Did You Hear"?

Did you hear about the wacky football
player who was really dumb?
No.
He once got lost in a huddle.

Did you hear the wacky joke about the
branding iron?
Not yet.
That joke is too hot to handle.

Did you hear the one about the wacky
amnesia patient?
I *don't think so.*
I forgot how it went.

Did you hear the wacky story about the
stupid kid?

Is it funny?
Yes, but I didn't get it.

Did you hear the wacky joke about the
   chocolate cake?
What happened?
You wouldn't get it—it's too rich.

Did you hear about the wacky rich kid
   who went to see Santa Claus?
Tell me.
He asked Santa what he needed for
   Christmas.

Did you hear the wacky joke about the
   little kid who wanted to buy a parrot?
No.
He didn't have enough money, so he
   bought a bird that was going cheep.

Did you hear the wacky joke about the
   fire at the shoe factory?
What about it?
150 soles were lost.

Did you hear the wacky joke about the
tramp?
Not yet.
It's a real bummer.

Did you hear about the wacky dog that
ate nothing but garlic?
I don't think so.
His bark was worse than his bite.

Did you hear the wacky joke about the ice
cube?
Is it funny?
It will leave you in the cold.

Did you hear about the wacky woman
who got carried away at a garage sale?
What happened?
She bought the whole garage.

Did you hear about the wacky woman
who got carried away at a garage sale?
What happened?
Someone bought her for $1.25.

Did you hear the wacky joke about the
    banana peel?
Tell me.
I would, but it slipped my mind.

Did you hear about the wacky man who
    went to a fire sale?
He tried to buy a fire!

Did you hear about the wacky man who
    was fired from his job in the drug
    store?
*He couldn't get the pill bottles into the
    typewriter.*

23
Winston & Wallace Wacky

Winston: What do you call a pig that took
an airplane ride?
Wallace: I have no clue.
Winston: Swine flu.

Winston: What do you call a sunburn on
your stomach?
Wallace: I don't know.
Winston: A pot roast.

Winston: What was the elephant doing in
the road?
Wallace: Beats me.
Winston: About three miles an hour.

Winston: What is Miss Piggy's life story?
Wallace: I can't guess.
Winston: A pigtail.

Winston: Which Chinese city is like a man
   looking through a keyhole?
Wallace: I have no idea.
Winston: Peking.

Winston: How does one dinosaur tell
   another one to hurry up?
Wallace: You tell me.
Winston: Pronto, Saurus!

Winston: What did the 300-pound mouse
   say?
Wallace: I give up.
Winston: Here kitty, kitty, kitty.

Winston: What weighs three tons, flies,
   and pulls Santa's sleigh?
Wallace: Who knows?
Winston: Rudolph the Red-Nosed
   Rhinoceros.

Winston: What do you call Batman and
   Robin after they get run over by a
   steam roller?
Wallace: You've got me.
Winston: Flatman and Ribbon.

Winston: When time flies, where does the
    pilot sit?
Wallace: My mind is a blank.
Winston: In the clockpit.

Winston: Why did Uncle Oscar name
    both of his sons Ed?
Wallace: That's a mystery.
Winston: Because he heard that two Eds
    are better than one.

Winston: What has four legs and flies?
Wallace: Tell me.
Winston: A pig.

Winston: What do you call a cow eating
    grass?
Wallace: I don't have the foggiest.
Winston: A lawn mooer.

Winston: Why don't cannibals eat
    clowns?
Wallace: It's unknown to me.
Winston: They taste funny.

Winston: What is purple and 5000 miles long?
Wallace: I'm in the dark.
Winston: The Grape Wall of China.

Winston: Why did Humpty-Dumpty fall off the wall?
Wallace: Search me.
Winston: To make the nursery rhyme go right.

Winston: What do you call a person who's mad about chocolate?
Wallace: You've got me guessing.
Winston: A coconut.

Winston: When does Kermit the Frog wake up?
Wallace: I'm not sure.
Winston: At the croak of dawn.

Winston: What do you call a crazy man who lives at the mouth of the Amazon?
Wallace: How should I know?
Winston: A Brazil nut.

Winston: What well-known animal drives
    an automobile?
Wallace: Give me the answer.
Winston: The road hog.

24
Whimsical Wacky Jokes

Cook: Do you want me to cut the pizza into six or eight pieces?

Wacky man: You'd better make it six. . . . I don't think I can eat eight pieces!

Teacher: What is an emperor?

Wacky scholar: I don't know.

Teacher: An emperor is a ruler.

Wacky scholar: Oh, sure; I used to carry an emperor to school with me.

Wacky wife: Honey, I can't get the car started. I think it's flooded.

Husband: Where is it?

Wacky wife: In the swimming pool.

Husband: It's flooded.

Wacky husband: Ouch! I bumped my
 crazy bone.
Wacky wife: Oh well, comb your hair right
 and the bump won't show.

Wacky boy: You could learn to love me,
 couldn't you?
Wacky girl: Well, I learned to eat spinach.

First wacky man: My wacky wife has been
 cooking a chicken for two days?
Second wacky man: For two days?
First wacky man: Yeah! The cookbook said
 to cook it one-half-hour to the
 pound . . . and my wife weighs 110
 pounds!

Then there was the wacky man who was
 so dumb that when he went to a mind
 reader she was forced to give him his
 money back.

This year the wacky family has taken to
 painting their garbage cans red and
 gold. Now their kids think they're
 eating at MacDonald's.

Wacky girl: Did Alice meet any wacky
characters on her trip through
Wonderland?
Wacky boy: Yes . . . Tweedle-dumb and
Tweedle-dumber.

Did you hear about the wacky secretary
who threw away her electric pencil
sharpener?
She didn't have any electric pencils!

25
Wigged-Out Wackys

Did you hear about the wacky man who
   won a gold medal in the Olympics?
He took it home and had it bronzed.

Did you hear about the wacky girl who
   found some milk bottles in the grass?
She thought she had found a cow's nest.

Did you hear about the wacky man who
   was going to have his head cut off?
*They put him on the block and pulled the trip
   cord. The blade came partway down and
   stopped. The wacky man said, "If you would
   oil that pulley, I think it would work better."*

Did you hear about the wacky woman
   who bought snow tires?
They melted the next day.

Did you hear about the wacky lawyer who
    was hurt in an accident?
The ambulance backed up suddenly.

Did you hear about the wacky man who
    locked his keys in his car?
It took him three hours to get his family out.

Did you hear about the wacky boy who
    bet $10 on a football game and lost?
*He bet $10 more on the instant replay and lost
    again.*

Did you hear about the wacky woman
    who went to the store for some
    birdseed?
"For which kind of bird?" asked the clerk.
"Oh, I dunno," replied the wacky woman.
    "Whichever kind will grow the fastest."

Did you hear about the wacky farmer who
    got killed by a cow?
It fell on him while he was getting a drink.

Why did the wacky boy cut a hole in his
   new umbrella?
So he could tell when it stops raining.

∽o∽

What did the wacky boy do when his boat
   sprung a leak at one end?
*He drilled a hole at the other end to let the
   water out.*

∽o∽

How did the employer of a large company
   know that he had hired a wacky
   secretary?
*There was white-out all over the computer
   screen.*

26
Walrus & Willis Wacky

Walrus: What is another name for income
tax?
Willis: I have no clue.
Walrus: Capital punishment.

Walrus: What do they call six women with
one luncheon check?
Willis: I don't know.
Walrus: Chaos.

Walrus: Name a very rude bird.
Willis: I can't.
Walrus: A mockingbird.

Walrus: What was the largest island before
Australia was discovered?
Willis: I can't guess.
Walrus: Australia.

Walrus: What do you do if you have cobwebs in your brain?
Willis: I have no idea.
Walrus: Use a vacuum cleaner.

Walrus: Who rode a dog and was a Confederate general during the Civil War?
Willis: You tell me.
Walrus: Robert E. Flea.

Walrus: What do you get if you cross a skeleton with a great detective?
Willis: I give up.
Walrus: Sherlock Bones.

Walrus: What do you call a stolen yam?
Willis: Who knows?
Walrus: Hot potato.

Walrus: What happened the week the TV set was broken?
Willis: You've got me.
Walrus: Seven days of silence.

Walrus: What did Old MacDonald see on
the chart when he took his eye test?
Willis: My mind is a blank.
Walrus: E-I-E-I-O.

Walrus: What happened to the duck that
flew upside down?
Willis: That's a mystery.
Walrus: It quacked up.

Walrus: What lives in the forest, puts out
fires, and has eight arms?
Willis: Tell me.
Walrus: Smokey Octopus.

Walrus: What happens to illegally parked
frogs?
Willis: I don't have the foggiest.
Walrus: They get toad away.

Walrus: Who always goes to sleep first?
Willis: It's unknown to me.
Walrus: The loudest snorer.

Walrus: What time is it when your clothes
wear out?

Willis: I'm in the dark.
Walrus: Ragtime.

❦

Walrus: What's the quickest way to collect on your life insurance?
Willis: Search me.
Walrus: Tell a hippo that his mother wears combat boots.

❦

Walrus: What do you call a person who wears neon shoes?
Willis: You've got me guessing.
Walrus: Twinkle toes.

❦

Walrus: What do you get when you put too much food in the oven?
Willis: I'm not sure.
Walrus: A pot-bellied stove.

❦

Walrus: What does a burglar feel when he climbs in a window and is greeted by a Great Dane?
Willis: How should I know?
Walrus: Burglar alarm.

❦

Walrus: What did people call Egg Foo
    when he was a little boy?
Willis: Give me the answer.
Walrus: Egg Foo Young.

27
Weird Wacky Jokes

Why do wacky families keep a doormat
    inside their house?
*So when they go outside they won't get the
    streets dirty.*

Friend: What kind of toothpaste do you
    use?
Wacky girl: I don't use any. My teeth
    aren't loose.

What did the wacky boy do with the
    hubcaps he stole?
He gave them to his mother to use for earrings.

Wacky student: Why did you tell every-
    one I was stupid?
Teacher: I'm sorry. I didn't know it was a
    secret.

Wacky mother: Why are you swimming
　　with your clothes on?
Wacky son: Because the water's cold.

How do you sink a wacky battleship?
Put it in the water.

Teacher: How do you spell Mississippi?
Wacky student: The river or the state?

Why does it take a wacky person five days
　　to wash his basement windows?
*He needs 4½ days to dig the holes for the
　　ladder.*

Wacky mother: Why on earth did you
　　swallow the money I gave you?
Wacky daughter: You said it was my lunch
　　money.

Why did the wacky couple want to get
　　married in the bathtub?
They wanted a double-ring ceremony.

What is the distance between a wacky
person's ears?
Next to nothing.

Did you hear about the wacky man who
was working as a carpenter? He was
nailing boards on the side of a house and
every now and then he would toss one
of the nails on the ground.

Wacky foreman: Why are you throwing all
those nails away?
Wacky carpenter: They're no good. The
heads are on the wrong side.
Wacky foreman: You idiot! They're for the
other side of the house.

28
More Wacky Definitions

What do they call dandruff?
Chips off the old block.

What is a drum?
An instrument you can't beat for noise.

What is a duck?
A chicken with snowshoes.

What do they call "humdinger"?
A person who hums while ringing a bell.

What do they call someone who jumps
onto other people's laps?
A laplander.

What do they call a "laugh"?
A smile that burst.

What do they call a one-liner?
A mini ha-ha.

What is overeating?
*An activity that will make you thick to your
  stomach.*

What is pig iron?
An iron for smoothing wrinkles off pigs.

What is a quack?
A doctor who ducks the law.

What's another name for rhubarb?
Bloodshot celery.

What do they call the punch a tired boxer
  throws?
A slowpoke.

What is stucco?
What you get when you sit on gummo.

What do they call a surfer?
Man-over-board.

What do they call "taxes"?
A place with a lot of cowboys.

What is a tricycle?
A tot rod.

What is the definition of "violin"?
*An instrument for musicians who like to fiddle
around.*

What is a walkie-talkie?
The opposite of sittie-stillie.

What will happen to you if you don't
know how to zwim?
They'll call you Zinc.

29

Warped Wackys

Customer: Give me two hot-dogs—one
with mustard and one without.
Wacky vendor: Which one without?

Wacky mother: Your face is clean, but how
did your hands get so dirty?
Wacky son: From washing my face.

What do you call a single wacky girl?
Nobody's fool.

What do you call a flea that lives in a
wacky person's ear?
A space invader.

Why do wacky people wear turtleneck
    sweaters?
To hide their flea collars.

Employer: Why are you so late to work?
Wacky employee: The escalator broke
    down, and I was stuck on it for over
    an hour.

What do they call a dance attended by a
    bunch of wacky students?
A goof ball.

Why does a wacky man need two hands
    to drink a bowl of soup?
*He has to hold one hand under the fork to
    catch the drippings.*

Wacky boy: What would I have to give
    you for one little kiss?
Wacky girl: Chloroform!

The doctor told the wacky boy to take
    medicine after a hot bath.
But he could barely finish drinking the bath!

Lady: I would like a pair of alligator shoes.
Wacky salesman: Yes, ma'am. What size is
   your alligator?

A wacky crook walked up to a man and
   said, "Stick 'em down."
The man replied, "You mean stick 'em up."
The wacky crook said, "No wonder I
   haven't made any money."

Judge: Order in this court! I'll have order
   in this court!
Wacky criminal: I'll have a hamburger
   with onions!

30
Winnett & Whittaker Wacky

Winnett: Do you know how long wacky cows should be milked?
Whittaker: Beats me.
Winnett: The same as short ones!

Winnett: How does a wacky dentist examine a crocodile's teeth?
Whittaker: I can't guess.
Winnett: Very carefully!

Winnett: Why wouldn't the wacky lightning bolt go to the storm?
Whittaker: I have no idea.
Winnett: Because it was on strike.

Winnett: Why did the wacky carpenter need a manicurist?

Whittaker: I don't know.
Winnett: To file his nails.

∽∘∽

Winnett: What do you call a wacky sheep
that hangs out with 40 thieves?
Whittaker: I have no idea.
Winnett: Ali Baa Baa.

∽∘∽

Winnett: What has an IQ of 192?
Whittaker: You tell me.
Winnett: A group of 100 wacky people.

∽∘∽

Winnett: What's the easiest job in the world?
Whittaker: I give up.
Winnett: The head of the Wacky
Intelligence Agency.

∽∘∽

Winnett: What happens to a wacky dog
who eats table scraps?
Whittaker: You've got me.
Winnett: He gets splinters in his tongue.

∽∘∽

Winnett: What kills wacky flies by sitting
on them?
Whittaker: My mind is a blank.
Winnett: A fly squatter.

❀

Winnett: What is purple and a wacky
    member of your family?
Whittaker: That's a mystery.
Winnett: Your grape grandmother.

❀

Winnett: What did the wacky cat say
    when his tail got caught in the
    lawnmower?
Whittaker: Tell me.
Winnett: It won't be long now.

❀

Winnett: What do they call a handsome,
    intelligent man in Wackyland?
Whittaker: I don't have the foggiest.
Winnett: A tourist.

❀

Winnett: What did the wacky stocking
    say to the needle?
Whittaker: I'm in the dark.
Winnett: I'll be darned!

❀

Winnett: What did wacky Jonah say when
    asked how he was feeling?
Whittaker: Search me.
Winnett: Very whale, thank you.

31
Webster & Waddington Wacky

Webster: What has three wacky feet but
no toes?
Waddington: Beats me.
Webster: A yardstick.

Webster: What has wacky arms but no
hands?
Waddington: I can't guess.
Webster: A chair.

Webster: Why did the wacky secret agent
take two aspirins and go to bed?
Waddington: I don't know.
Webster: He had a code in his head.

Webster: What did wacky Bambi put on
the back of his car?

Waddington: I have no idea.
Webster: A Thumpersticker.

Webster: What does a wacky vet keep
  outside his front door?
Waddington: You tell me.
Webster: A welcome mutt.

Webster: What do you have in December
  that you don't have in any other month?
Waddington: I give up.
Webster: The letter D.

Webster: What do wacky jigsaw puzzles
  do when they get bad news?
Waddington: Who knows?
Webster: Go to pieces.

Webster: What do you call a wacky couple
  of salesmen who get sent to jail?
Waddington: You've got me.
Webster: Sell-mates.

Webster: What happens when you fall in
  love with a wacky jogger?

Waddington: That's a mystery.
Webster: You get the run-around.

∽o∾

Webster: What would you call a wacky
    bird that joins the Ice Capades?
Waddington: Tell me.
Webster: A cheep-skate.

∽o∾

Webster: What's the use of wacky reindeer
    (rain, dear)?
Waddington: I don't have the foggiest.
Webster: It makes the little flowers grow.

∽o∾

Webster: Why did the wacky secret agent
    whisper 1, 2, 3, 4, 5, 6, 7, etc. ?
Waddington: It's unknown to me.
Webster: He was a counter-spy.

∽o∾

Webster: What wacky state doesn't feel
    good?
Waddington: I'm in the dark.
Webster: Ill.

∽o∾

Webster: What grows on a tree and is
    terrified of wolves?

Waddington: Search me.
Webster: The Three Little Figs.

Webster: What happened when the wacky
    musician died?
Waddington: You've got me guessing.
Webster: He decomposed.

32

Wentworth &
Woodbury Wacky

Wentworth: What grows larger the more
you take away?
Woodbury: Beats me.
Wentworth: A hole.

Wentworth: How can you change a wacky
pumpkin into another vegetable?
Woodbury: I can't guess.
Wentworth: Throw it down on the ground
and it will become squash.

Wentworth: Why did Mr. and Mrs. Wacky
Cat get married?
Woodbury: I have no clue.
Wentworth: They were a purr-fect match.

Wentworth: Why didn't wacky Wilma like the joke about the Grand Canyon?
Woodbury: I don't know.
Wentworth: It was too deep.

❧❧❧

Wentworth: What wacky bear never bathes?
Woodbury: I have know idea.
Wentworth: Winnie-the-Phew.

❧❧❧

Wentworth: What wacky cow jumps off buildings for fun?
Woodbury: You tell me.
Wentworth: A dairy devil.

❧❧❧

Wentworth: What would you get if you crossed a wacky dentist with a military officer?
Woodbury: I give up.
Wentworth: A drill sergeant.

❧❧❧

Wentworth: What wacky cowboy never said a word?
Woodbury: Who knows?
Wentworth: Quiet Earp.

❧❧❧

Wentworth: What do you get from a wacky, very forgetful cow?
Woodbury: You've got me.
Wentworth: Milk of Amnesia.

Wentworth: What do you get from a wacky, very funny cow?
Woodbury: My mind is a blank.
Wentworth: Cream of wit.

Wentworth: What happened to wacky Little Bo Peep after she spent all day looking for her sheep?
Woodbury: That's a mystery.
Wentworth: She was Little Bo Pooped.

Wentworth: What wacky snowstorm covered the Emerald City?
Woodbury: Tell me.
Wentworth: The Blizzard of Oz.

Wentworth: What do wacky sharks eat with their peanut butter?
Woodbury: I don't have the foggiest.
Wentworth: Jellyfish.

Wentworth: What do you get if you cross
  a wacky sheep and a monkey?
Woodbury: It's unknown to me.
Wentworth: A baa-boon.

⌣○⌣

Wentworth: What's the name of the
  world's best known waterfall?
Woodbury: I'm in the dark.
Wentworth: Rain.

⌣○⌣

Wentworth: What happens to wacky
  spoons when they work too hard?
Woodbury: Search me.
Wentworth: They go stir crazy!

33
Waddell & Waldorf Wacky

Waddell: What can you hold without
touching it?
Waldorf: Beats me.
Waddell: Your breath.

Waddell: What is the best way to kill
time?
Waldorf: I can't guess.
Waddell: Work it to death.

Waddell: Why was the wacky calendar so
sad?
Waldorf: I have no clue.
Waddell: Its days were numbered.

Waddell: Why was the wacky duck un-
happy?

Waldorf: I don't know.
Waddell: His bill was in the mail.

❧

Waddell: What is a wacky frog asked
  when he comes into a restaurant?
Waldorf: I have no idea.
Waddell: Croaking or non-croaking?

❧

Waddell: What kind of wacky house
  weighs the least?
Waldorf: You tell me.
Waddell: A lighthouse.

❧

Waddell: What is green, red, orange,
  chartreuse, purple, brown, pink,
  and covered with polka dots?
Waldorf: I give up.
Waddell: A wacky woman dressed up for
  church.

❧

Waddell: What does it say on the bottom
  of Coke bottles in Wackyland?
Waldorf: Who knows?
Waddell: Open other end.

❧

Waddell: What do you call a wacky hot
dog who always speaks his mind?
Waldorf: You've got me.
Waddell: A frankfurter.

Waddell: What time is it when twelve
wacky dogs chase a cat?
Waldorf: My mind is a blank.
Waddell: Twelve after one.

Waddell: What do wacky mechanics do in
aerobics class?
Waldorf: That's a mystery.
Waddell: Touch their tow-trucks.

Waddell: What did the wacky Atlantic
Ocean say to the Pacific Ocean?
Waldorf: Tell me.
Waddell: Nothing, it just waved.

Waddell: What wacky turkey starred in
Gone with the Wind?
Waldorf: I don't have the foggiest.
Waddell: Clark Gobble.

Waddell: What was Wacky Chicken
    Souperman's other name?
Waldorf: It's unknown to me.
Waddell: Cluck Kent.

∞◦∞

Waddell: What's worse than a wacky
    turtle with claustrophobia?
Waldorf: I'm in the dark.
Waddell: An elephant with hay fever.

∞◦∞

Waddell: What practical jokes do wacky
    mathematicians play?
Waldorf: Search me.
Waddell: Arithmetricks.

34

Wilhelmina & Winchel Wacky

Wilhelmina: When can you spell wacky
with one letter?
Winchel: Beats me.
Wilhelmina: When it's U!

Wilhelmina: Which wacky traffic light is
the bravest?
Winchel: I can't guess.
Wilhelmina: The one that doesn't turn
yellow.

Wilhelmina: Why did the wacky frog sit
on the lily pad?
Winchel: I have no clue.
Wilhelmina: Her sofa was being repaired.

Wilhelmina: Why did the wacky frog get kicked out of the navy?
Winchel: I don't know.
Wilhelmina: He kept jumping ship.

Wilhelmina: What are the odds of something wacky happening at 12:50 P.M.?
Winchel: I have no idea.
Wilhelmina: Ten-to-one.

Wilhelmina: What's the biggest soda in the world?
Winchel: You tell me.
Wilhelmina: Minnesota.

Wilhelmina: What's purple, lives in the jungle, and is always on a vine?
Winchel: I give up.
Wilhelmina: Tarzan the Grape Man.

Wilhelmina: What happens to wacky dogs who chase cars?
Winchel: Who knows?
Wilhelmina: They end up exhausted.

Wilhelmina: What cultivates the earth
  and gives milk?
Winchel: You've got me.
Wilhelmina: Bossie the Plow.

Wilhelmina: What does a wacky Eskimo
  put on his bed?
Winchel: My mind is a blank.
Wilhelmina: A sheet of ice and a blanket
  of snow.

Wilhelmina: What has brown fur, wears a
  ranger's hat, and hangs from a tree?
Winchel: That's a mystery.
Wilhelmina: Smokey the Pear.

Wilhelmina: What's another name for a
  wacky dining car?
Winchel: Tell me.
Wilhelmina: A chew-chew train.

Wilhelmina: What is orange and half a
  mile high?
Winchel: I don't have the foggiest.
Wilhelmina: The Empire State Carrot.

Wilhelmina: What did you do last summer?
Winchel: I worked for an elevator
    company.
Wilhelmina: I'll bet that had its ups and
    downs.

Wilhelmina: What wacky state is a doctor?
Winchel: I'm in the dark.
Wilhelmina: MD.

Wilhelmina: What wacky fruit studies for
    exams in a hurry?
Winchel: Search me.
Wilhelmina: Cramberries.

35
Wiebe & Wella Wacky

Wiebe: What is found in the center of America and Australia?
Wella: Beats me.
Wiebe: The letter R.

∽◦∾

Wiebe: What are 365 periods of disappointment called?
Wella: I can't guess.
Wiebe: A year.

∽◦∾

Wiebe: Why didn't wacky Eve have any sisters?
Wella: I have no clue.
Wiebe: Because Adam had no spare ribs.

∽◦∾

Wiebe: Why is it a good idea to have holes in your jeans?
Wella: I don't know.

Wiebe: So that you can get your legs
    inside.

Wiebe: What's a wacky cat's skin used for?
Wella: I have no idea.
Wiebe: To hold the cat together.

Wiebe: What climbs trees, stores nuts for
    the winter, and weighs three tons?
Wella: I give up.
Wiebe: A wacky elephant who thinks he's
    a squirrel.

Wiebe: What wacky locomotive wears
    sneakers?
Wella: Who knows?
Wiebe: A shoe-shoe train.

Wiebe: What kind of wacky car did Elsie
    the Cow drive?
Wella: My mind is a blank.
Wiebe: A moo-ving van.

Wiebe: What do you call great bodies of
    water filled with grape juice?

Wella: That's a mystery.
Wiebe: The Grape Lakes.

<hr/>

Wiebe: What do wacky patriotic monkeys
    wave on Flag Day?
Wella: Tell me.
Wiebe: Star Spangled Bananas.

<hr/>

Wiebe: What's harder than catching a
    wacky train when you're late?
Wella: I don't have the foggiest.
Wiebe: Throwing one.

<hr/>

Wiebe: What happens to wacky Whistler's
    mother when she works too hard?
Wella: It's unknown to me.
Wiebe: She goes off her rocker.

<hr/>

Wiebe: What wacky state is necessary for
    dirty clothes?
Wella: I'm in the dark.
Wiebe: Wash.

<hr/>

Wiebe: What do you call it when you holler
    to a wacky person two miles away?
Wella: Search me.
Wiebe: Lung distance.

36

Wamsley & Willa Wacky

Wamsley: Who was the famous chicken
who rode with the wacky Rough
Riders and later became president?
Willa: Beats me.
Wamsley: Teddy Roostervelt.

Wamsley: Where do wacky frogs hang up
their coats?
Willa: I can't guess.
Wamsley: In the croak room.

Wamsley: Why did wacky Elsie the Cow
go to Hollywood?
Willa: I have no clue.
Wamsley: To be a moo-vie star.

Wamsley: Why don't wacky rabbits carry calculators?

Willa: I don't know.

Wamsley: Because they multiply so quickly without them.

Wamsley: What wacky word of three syllables is always mispronounced?

Willa: I have no idea.

Wamsley: Mispronounced.

Wamsley: What wacky game do rabbits always love to play?

Willa: You tell me.

Wamsley: Hopscotch.

Wamsley: What's black and white and pink all over?

Willa: I give up.

Wamsley: An embarrassed zebra.

Wamsley: What wacky business is King Kong in?

Willa: Who knows?

Wamsley: Monkey business.

Wamsley: What do wacky, short, fairy-tale characters wear to look taller?
Willa: You've got me.
Wamsley: Rumple-stilts.

Wamsley: What wacky dancer spins straw into gold?
Willa: My mind is a blank.
Wamsley: Rhumba-stiltskin.

Wamsley: What wacky cowboy steals teapots?
Willa: That's a mystery.
Wamsley: A kettle rustler.

Wamsley: What did wacky Ali Baba write on?
Willa: Tell me.
Wamsley: Sandpaper.

Wamsley: What state do you use when you talk about yourself?
Willa: I don't have the foggiest.
Wamsley: ME.

Wamsley: What state would a gold pros-
  pector like?
Willa: It's unknown to me.
Wamsley: Ore.

∽o∽

Wamsley: What state is a church service?
Willa: I'm in the dark.
Wamsley: Mass.

∽o∽

Wamsley: What did wacky Sir Lancelot
  wear to bed?
Willa: Search me.
Wamsley: A knightgown.

37

Wellington & Wenonah Wacky

Wellington: Why wouldn't the wacky
otter cross the road?
Wenonah: Beats me.
Wellington: He didn't want to be
mistaken for a chicken.

∽◦∾

Wellington: Why couldn't the wacky crab
learn to share?
Wenonah: I can't guess.
Wellington: Because it was shellfish.

∽◦∾

Wellington: What's the difference between
a wacky lizard, a crybaby, and the
Roadrunner?
Wenonah: I don't know.
Wellington: One creeps, one weeps, and
one beeps.

Wellington: What did the wacky thief
  name his son?
Wenonah: I have no idea.
Wellington: Robin.

Wellington: What can't you hold for half
  an hour—even though it's lighter than
  air?
Wenonah: You tell me.
Wellington: Your breath.

Wellington: What wacky ape helped settle
  the American frontier?
Wenonah: I give up.
Wellington: Daniel Ba-Boone.

Wellington: What do you find in a wacky
  pig mall?
Wenonah: You've got me.
Wellington: Pork shops.

Wellington: What do 500-pound wacky
  canaries do on Sundays?
Wenonah: My mind is a blank.
Wellington: They go to chirp.

Wellington: What is the best-looking geometric figure?
Wenonah: That's a mystery.
Wellington: Acute angle.

Wellington: What do you get when you use wacky soap and water on the stove?
Wenonah: Tell me.
Wellington: Foam on the range.

Wellington: What is the wackiest and cheapest way to buy holes?
Wenonah: I don't have the foggiest.
Wellington: Wholesale.

Wellington: What is the earth's wackiest satellite?
Wenonah: It's unknown to me.
Wellington: A fool moon.

38

Wadsworth &
Whitmore Wacky

Wadsworth: When does a wacky farmer
have the best chance to see his pigs?
Whitmore: You've got me guessing.
Wadsworth: When he has a sty on his eye.

Wadsworth: Why does a wacky elephant
like peanuts?
Whitmore: I'm not sure.
Wadsworth: Because it can send in the
wrappers for prizes.

Wadsworth: Why did the wacky fish get
turned down by the army?
Whitmore: How should I know?
Wadsworth: He failed his herring test.

Wadsworth: What wacky shampoo do mountains use?
Whitmore: Give me the answer.
Wadsworth: Head and Boulders.

∽o∼

Wadsworth: What do you get when you cross a wacky lighthouse and a henhouse?
Whitmore: Beats me.
Wadsworth: Beacon and eggs.

∽o∼

Wadsworth: What does a wacky near-sighted gingerbread man use for eyes?
Whitmore: I can't guess.
Wadsworth: Contact raisins.

∽o∼

Wadsworth: What do you get when you cross a wacky movie and a swimming pool?
Whitmore: I have no clue.
Wadsworth: A dive-in theater.

∽o∼

Wadsworth: What part of the wacky car is first to get weary?
Whitmore: I don't know.
Wadsworth: The tire.

∽o∼

Wadsworth: What's yellow, swims in the
  ocean, and swallows ships?
Whitmore: I have no idea.
Wadsworth: Moby Banana.

∿∘∿

Wadsworth: What did the wacky adding
  machine say to the clerk?
Whitmore: You tell me.
Wadsworth: You can count on me.

∿∘∿

Wadsworth: What did the wacky apple
  tree say to the farmer?
Whitmore: I give up.
Wadsworth: Why don't you stop picking
  on me?

∿∘∿

Wadsworth: What is the smallest building
  in all of Wackyland?
Whitmore: Who knows?
Wadsworth: The Hall of Fame.

∿∘∿

Wadsworth: What do wacky ravens sail
  in?
Whitmore: That's a mystery.
Wadsworth: Crowboats.

39
Whale of a Tale of Wackys

I have a mouth, but no teeth. What am I?
A river.

Who is the first wacky Irishman you see
    in the spring?
Paddy O'Furniture.

How do wacky baby birds learn how to
    fly?
They just sort of wing it.

How do wacky soldiers sleep out in the
    open?
*In beds of flowers, on sheets of rain, and under
    blankets of fog.*

What's located beneath your wacky nose?
Tulips.

If she married wacky Mr. Hill who's
brother had children, what would she
become?
Ant Hill.

If your wacky aunt had rabbit ears, what
would she be?
Antenna.

What does a wacky hen do just before she
stands on one foot?
She lifts up the other one.

What do they call someone with a wacky
burning desire?
An arsonist.

What is another name for a wacky ma-
ternity dress?
A spacesuit.

Why would you expect a wacky fisherman
 to be more honest than a shepherd?
*Because a fisherman lives by hook and a
 shepherd lives by crook.*

What's the most wacky and popular
 gardening magazine?
Weeder's Digest.

What makes a wacky empty matchbox
 superior to any other?
It is matchless.

How often do wacky big ocean liners sink?
Only once.

When is it bad luck to have a wacky black
 cat follow you?
When you are a mouse.

40
More Walloping Wackys

Where does wacky Mother Goose leave
    her garbage?
At the Humpty Dump.

Who haunts the Sahara Desert?
The sandwich.

Who helped wacky Cinderella's cat go to
    the ball?
Its furry godmother.

Which wacky president talked like a pig?
Ulysses S. Grunt.

Where do wacky dieters go on vacation?
Hungary.

What do you get when you cross wacky
    peanuts with golf balls?
Peanut putters.

Do you know the wacky joke about the
    oil?
Well, I won't tell you. It's too crude.

What happened when the wacky dog
    visited the flea circus?
He stole the show.

Why does a wacky hen lay an egg?
Because she can't lay a brick.

Why is it hard to talk with a wacky goat
    around?
Because he always butts in.

Can you spell mousetrap in three letters?
C-A-T.

I came to town and met three wacky
people. They were neither men, nor
women, nor children. What were
they?
A man, a woman, and a child.

What wacky animal has the highest level
of intelligence?
The giraffe.

What is so brittle that it can be broken
just by naming it?
Silence.

What do they call a wacky smoking
mathematician?
A puff adder.

What kind of wacky sea creature is like an
expression of disbelief?
Abalone.

41
Wagonful of Wackys

What is black and white and red all over?
A zebra with a sunburn.

Why are wacky oysters lazy?
Because they are always found in beds.

What kind of ears does a wacky engine
   have?
Engineers.

Where does a wacky Ken doll grill his
   hamburgers?
At a Barbie-cue.

How can you tell if your wacky lawn is
   sick?
When you hear the grass mown.

When the wacky baby cries at night, who gets up?
The whole neighborhood.

What is a conversation among wacky dogs called?
A bowwow powwow.

What is a stupid ruler called?
A ding-a-ling king.

What two letters got kicked out of the wacky alphabet for being rotten?
D–K.

Who is Mexico's most famous fat man?
Pauncho Villa.

When does a wacky girl admire a bachelor's voice?
When there is a ring in it.

What's the best way to find out what a
    wacky woman thinks of you?
Marry her.

Why do wacky hummingbirds hum?
Because they can't remember the words.

42
Wackys Welcome

What makes more noise than a wacky pig
in a sty?
Two pigs.

∽∘∾

How do you top a wacky car?
Tep on the brake, toopid!

∽∘∾

Which wacky fruit is always sad?
Blueberries.

∽∘∾

Where do wacky peroxide blondes sit at
baseball games?
In the bleachers.

∽∘∾

I have leaves, but I'm not a plant. What
am I?
A table.

What's wacky, hard-boiled, and can
benchpress 300 pounds?
Arnold Schwarzenegg.

With what two wacky animals do you
always go to bed?
Two calves.

What do you call a deep valley with high
slopes that is worth a thousand
dollars?
Grand Canyon.

What is the difference between a wacky
engineer and a teacher?
*One minds the train, while the other trains
the mind.*

What do you do with a wacky blue
monster?
Cheer him up.

What country makes you shiver with cold?
Chile.

What wacky fish is man's best friend?
The dogfish.

What do you call the secret instructions
for opening a zipper?
Zip Code.

Why was wacky Cleopatra so hard to get
along with?
She was the queen of denial.

Name a wacky carpenter's tool you can
spell forward and backward the same
way.
Level.

43
Way-Out Wackys

What can overpower a wacky karate
   master without hurting him?
Sleep.

Where do wacky plants grow?
In crackpots.

Why doesn't the wacky sheik get married?
Harum-scarum.

How many letters are in the wacky
   alphabet?
Eleven. T-H-E A-L-P-H-A-B-E-T.

What kind of wacky dress do you have
   but never wear?
Your address.

Why do wacky single girls like the moon?
Because there's a man in it.

What wacky vegetable do you find in
  crowded streetcars and buses?
Squash.

What do you do when you want to take a
  pole from one place to another?
Totem pole.

What has no feet but always wears shoes?
The sidewalk.

What does the wacky envelope say when
  you lick it?
It just shuts up and says nothing.

To what question must you positively
  answer yes?
What does Y-E-S spell?

Why is a wacky pig in your kitchen like a
house on fire?
The sooner it's put out the better.

44

Warped Wackys

Who sings "Love Me Tender" and makes
wacky Christmas toys?
Santa's little Elvis.

What is the right kind of timber for wacky
castles in the air?
Sunbeams.

How did the prime minister of Wackyland
deal with the problem of Red China?
He bought a pink tablecloth.

Why do wacky people have scratched
faces on Monday mornings?
*Because they eat with knives and forks over the
weekend.*

Which season do wacky kangaroos like the best?
Springtime!

∽o∽

Where are ankles located?
Overshoes.

∽o∽

What do you call a wacky raccoon that wears bow ties?
Tycoon.

∽o∽

What do you call it if your wacky toes have a good cry?
Football.

∽o∽

Why is E the most unfortunate of all the letters?
Because it is never in cash, always in debt, and never out of danger.

∽o∽

What two wacky numbers multiplied together make 13?
1 and 13.

∽o∽

Where do wacky fish keep their life
    savings?
In a riverbank.

Why shouldn't wacky American girls learn
    Russian?
Because one tongue is enough for any girl.

What gets lost every time you stand up?
Your lap.

If a soft answer turns away wrath, what
    does a hard answer do?
It turns wrath your way.

How can you tell a wacky Jersey cow from
    any other cow?
By its license plate.

What's the longest word in the dictionary?
*Smiles. There's a mile between the first and last
    letter.*

45

More Wigged-Out Wackys

What is smaller than a wacky ant's
   mouth?
His teeth.

∞◦∞

How does a wacky person spell farm?
E-I-E-I-O.

∞◦∞

How does a wacky train conductor
   sneeze?
Ahhhh choo-choo!

∞◦∞

How can you recognize wacky rabbit
   stew?
It has hares in it.

∞◦∞

How many wacky actors does it take to change a lightbulb?
100. One to change it and 99 to stand around and say, "I could have done that."

❦

What goes putt-putt-putt-putt?
An over-par golfer.

❦

What two wacky things can you never eat for breakfast?
Lunch and dinner.

❦

Why did the wacky little boy go to sleep with birds in his shoes?
He wanted to feed his pigeon-toes.

❦

How should you greet a wacky German barber?
Herr Dresser.

❦

Why is a wacky ex-boxer like a beehive?
An ex-boxer is an ex-pounder; an expounder is a commentator; a common tater is an Irish tater; an Irish tater is a speck'd tater; a spectator is a beholder; and a beeholder is a beehive.

Which is larger: wacky Mr. Larger or
  wacky Mr. Larger's baby?
The baby is a little Larger.

What do you call someone who steals
  pigs?
A hamburglar.

If joy is the opposite of sorrow, what is the
  opposite of woe?
Giddyap!

What did one wacky elevator say to the
  other wacky elevator?
I think I'm coming down with something.

46
Wacky Whoops!

What is the difference between a wacky
   mouse and a young lady?
*One harms the cheese, and the other charms the
   he's.*

 ∽o∽

How does a wacky person fan himself?
*Holds his hand still and waves his face in front
   of it.*

 ∽o∽

Which is heavier: a half moon or a full moon?
A half moon because the full moon is lighter.

 ∽o∽

What is a successful criminal?
A smug thug.

 ∽o∽

What is an insane flower?
A crazy daisy.

What kind of wacky sentence would you get if you broke the law of gravity?
A suspended one.

Do wacky chickens jog?
No, but turkeys trot.

Who is the oldest whistler in the world?
The wind.

What is it that has never killed anybody but seems to scare some people half to death?
Work.

If an apple a day keeps the wacky doctor away, what does an onion do?
It keeps everybody away!

What is the Wackiest and oldest tree?
The elder.

Why didn't the wacky baby get hurt when
he fell down?
Because he was wearing safety pins.

47
Walleyed Wackys

Which wacky shoes are made for lazy
people?
Loafers.

Was wacky Ben Franklin surprised when
he discovered electricity?
Oh yes! He was shocked.

When wacky fish swim in schools, who
helps out the teacher?
The herring aide.

When does wacky rainfall make mistakes?
During a blunderstorm.

What happens when the wacky bridge of
your nose collapses?
Nose drops.

Why couldn't the wacky pony talk?
He was a little hoarse.

Do wacky fish sing?
Only when they have musical scales.

Why did the wacky shrimp blush?
Because somebody saw it in the salad dressing.

Why was it that after wacky Mrs. Jones
gave her neighbor a butter churn, her
neighbor gave her one back?
One good churn deserves another.

Why is an empty purse always the same?
Because there is never any change in it.

Why does a wacky elephant wear
sunglasses?
*If you were the one they were telling all these
jokes about, you would want to hide too!*

If a wacky farmer sold 500 bushels of
　　wheat for a dollar a bushel, what
　　would he get?
A lot of customers.

If one wacky horse is shut up in a stable
　　and another one is running loose
　　down the road, which horse is singing
　　"Don't Fence Me In"?
Neither! Horses can't sing.

What will change a wacky pear into a
　　pearl?
The letter L.

What do you call a wacky veterinarian
　　with laryngitis?
A hoarse doctor.

What would a wacky cannibal be if he ate
　　his mother's sister?
An aunt eater.

48

More Wacky Wit

How do you cheer for a wacky basketball player?
Hoop Hoop Hooray!

What day of the year is a command to go forward?
March 4th.

How do you revive a wacky butterfly that has fainted?
With moth-to-moth resuscitation.

Who invents wacky telephones and carries your luggage?
Alexander Graham Bellhop.

What would you get if you dropped
 chocolate on the beach?
Sandy candy.

If a wacky man married a princess, what
 would he be?
Her husband.

What is the best way to keep a wacky
 skunk from smelling?
Hold his nose.

When was wacky beef the highest it has
 ever been?
When the cow jumped over the moon.

What did the wacky Eskimo shout to his
 dogs Corn and Meal?
Cornmeal mush.

If all the money in the world were divided
 equally among wacky people, how
 much would each person get?
An equal amount.

What do they call a wacky dollar with all
the taxes taken out?
A nickel.

What kind of wacky jokes does a scholar
make?
Wisecracks.

If the wacky man you work for weighs
2000 pounds, what do you call him?
Boston (Boss ton).

What is the best day to fry wacky food?
Friday.

What two opposites mean the same thing?
Half-full and half-empty.

49

Washed-Out Wackys

Did you hear about the wacky football captain who didn't believe he lost the coin toss?
He demanded to see it again on instant replay.

When five wacky men fell in the water, why did only four of them get their hair wet?
Because one of them was bald.

How can you tell when a wacky tree is really frightened?
It'll be petrified.

Sign on a newly seeded lawn: *Your feet are killing me!*

Sign in a wacky old-age home: *We're not deaf. We just heard everything worth hearing already.*

Sign in a wacky shop window: *Wanted: Clerk to work eight hours a day to replace one who didn't.*

Sign in a wacky delicatessen window: *Come in for a hello and good buys.*

Sign in a wacky ice cream shop: *You can't beat our milk shakes, but you can lick our ice cream cones.*

A wacky rope tried to enlist in the army, but the recruiting sergeant rejected it on sight. No ropes allowed, he said.

The wacky rope went home, tied itself into a big knot, and frayed both its ends. The next day the wacky rope returned to the recruiting office.

"Hey, aren't you the wacky rope that tried to enlist yesterday?" asked the sergeant.

"No," said the wacky rope, "I'm a frayed knot."

∽∘∾

A wacky boss: *A man who is at the office early on the days when you're late.*

∽∘∾

If you breathe oxygen in the daytime, what do you breathe in the nighttime? *Nitrogen, of course!*

∽∘∾

"Have you ever seen a wacky catfish?"
"Of course."
"How did he hold the pole?"

∽∘∾

Wacky Cleaver: I was once a 90-pound weakling. When I went to the beach, a 200-pound bully kicked sand in my face. That was the end. I exercised every day and in a little while I weighed 200-pounds.
Wendy: Then what happened?
Wacky Cleaver: I went to the beach and a 400-pound bully kicked sand in my face!

∽∘∾

Sign in a wacky egg factory: *Fowl play not allowed.*

∽∘∾

Sergeant: So you're complaining about a
little sand in your soup?

Wacky private: Yes, sir.

Sergeant: Did you join the army to serve
your country or complain about the
food?

Wacky private: I joined the army to serve
my country, not to eat it.

❧

Wacky Collette: A very strange thing
happened to me out in the street. A
bum came up to me and asked me for
a quarter to eat.

Wanda: That's not strange. Bums do that
all the time. Did you give him a
quarter?

Wacky Collette: Yeah. And he ate it!

❧

Three little kittens were born to a wacky
Fresno family named Wests. The first
had one black foot. The second kitten
had two black feet. The third had
three black feet. So the family named
them Foot, Foot Foot, and Foot Foot
Foot.

One day the little West girl took the
kittens to the beach and tragedy
struck. A wave washed one of the
kittens away. The girl rushed home
sobbing.

"Which one did you lose?" asked Mrs. West.

"Foot," replied the girl.

"I hope you've learned your lesson," said her mother. "Don't ever take those kittens back to the beach again."

"Why not?" asked the girl.

"Because we've already got one Foot in the grave!" replied her mother.

Instead of bringing the teacher an apple every day, wacky David, the baker's son, brought her a pretzel. One day she said to him, "These pretzels are very good, but please tell your dad that they're a little too salty for me."

The next day, she received a pretzel with no salt at all. From then on the pretzels arrived without salt. A month later she said to wacky Bobby, "I hope your father doesn't go to too much trouble making these pretzels without salt."

"He doesn't make 'em without salt," said the boy. "I lick it off."

Sign in a wacky pawnshop: *See us at your earliest inconvenience.*

Wacky St. Peter greeted a lawyer at the
  pearly gates with unusual warmth.
"Gee," said the lawyer, "does everybody
  get this kind of treatment?"
"You're not just anyone," wacky St. Peter
  replied. "We seldom get lawyers who
  are as distinguished and old as you."
"But I'm only 48," the lawyer said.
"Funny," wacky St. Peter said. "You've
  billed for so many hours we thought
  you were 80!"

50

Warehouse Full of Wackys

What is the biggest handicap in golf?
Honesty.

How many wacky people does it require to take a picture off the wall?
Ten. One to hold the picture and nine to knock down the wall.

Where do wacky king crabs live?
In sand castles.

Who changed wacky King Tut's diapers?
His mummy.

I have ears but I can't hear. What am I?
A cornstalk.

What does everybody give and few take?
Advice.

What is the difference between a wacky
  elephant and a flea?
*A wacky elephant can have fleas, but a flea
  can't have elephants.*

How do you remove varnish?
Take out the "r" and make it vanish.

What age do most wacky girls wish to
  attain?
Marriage.

What do you call a wacky prankster who
  eats chili peppers for dinner?
A hot time in the old clown tonight.

What's the difference between a wacky
  lawyer and a vulture?
Frequent-flier miles.

What do wacky hippopotamuses have that
  no other animals have?
Baby hippopotamuses.

What is the value of the moon?
Four quarters.

51

A Whirlwind of Wackys

Do you know why wacky people only get
half an hour off for lunch?
If they had an hour, they'd have to be retrained.

"We picked some of your apples," yelled
the motorist as he drove away from
the wacky farmer's orchard. "We
didn't think you'd mind."
"Not at all," yelled the wacky farmer after
them. "I picked some of your car's
tools from the trunk. I didn't think
you'd mind either."

Mother: You should eat your vegetables.
Green things are good for you.
Wacky Cramer: Couldn't I have Lime
Sherbert ice cream instead?

Sign on a vegetable stand: *Our corn will
tickle your taste buds and make you smile
from ear to ear.*

Why isn't that man allowed to visit the
zoo anymore?
His face scares all of the animals away.

Wanda: Write something on a piece of
paper.
Windy: Okay, what next?
Wanda: Fold it, put it on the floor, and
put your foot on it.
Windy: Okay, now what?
Wanda: I can tell you what is on the paper.
Windy: What?
Wanda: Your foot.

Was the blimp wacky?
Yes, it was a balloonatic.

Whimsey: Ouch! I just got a lump on my
head.
Willy: That's swell.

Street sweeper: Did it hurt when the street lamp fell on your head?

Wacky street cleaner: No, it was a light pole.

A wacky buddy of mine was always being kept after school. He spent so much time at school, they delivered his mail there.

Wholly: The doctor's helping me lose weight with these three pills. This red one's for before dinner. That green one's for after dinner.

Wendell: And what's the pink one for?

Wholly: The pink one *is* dinner.

Sign in a power generator plant: *We have the power to make you see the light.*

Wacky handyman: I need 36 two-by-fours.

Salesclerk: How long?

Wacky handyman: Oh, a long time. I'm building a house!

He was so dumb he thought a Band-Aid was a charitable organization for musicians.

Golfer: You're such a lousy caddy! When we get back to the clubhouse I'm going to see that you get fired.

Wacky caddy: It's okay with me. By the time we get back to the clubhouse I'll be old enough to get a regular job!

52

Whoopee!
More Wackys!

How many sides does a circle have?
Two. Inside and outside.

Why don't they let wacky people operate
    elevators?
They forget the route.

Who serves a four-year term of office,
    signs documents, and rattles?
The president of the United Snakes.

How do wacky amoebas break up with
    their girlfriends?
They split.

What does bigmouth William do when he
hears a secret?
William Tell.

Name two people who were never wrong?
Wilbur and Orville Wright.

When do you put a mouse in your wacky
sister's bed?
When you can't find a frog.

What colors would you paint the sun and
the wind?
The sun rose and the wind blue.

When a wacky librarian goes fishing, what
does she use for bait?
Bookworms.

What did one wacky horse say to the
other?
*I can't remember your mane but your pace is
familiar.*

Why should a wacky man never tell his secrets in a cornfield?
Because there are too many ears there, and they might be shocked.

❦

Which is the best side of the bed to sleep on?
The top side.

❦

What did one stuck-up person say to another?
Nothing.

❦

How can you be sure the engine in your car isn't missing?
Lift the hood and look.

53

Wacky Doctors

Doc, one night I dreamed I was in a wigwam, the next night I dreamed I was living in a teepee. What's happening to me?
Nothing. You're just too tents.

Doc, what's your best suggestion for this terrible bad breath of mine?
Lockjaw.

Doc, what should I do? I can't sleep at night.
Sleep during the day.

Patient: Doc, what do you charge for a visit?
Doctor: I charge $50 for the first visit and $25 for each visit thereafter.

Patient: Well I'm here again.
Doctor: Fine, take the same thing as last time.

Doc, this ointment you gave me makes my arm smart.
Why not rub some on your head?

A worried mother: Doctor, my little boy just swallowed a bottle of ink. What should I do?
Doctor: Try to get him to swallow an ink blotter!

Wacky patient: My doctor classified me as a workaholic and suggested I get psychiatric treatment.
Friend: So what did you do?
Wacky patient: I got another job so I could afford a psychiatrist.

Two wacky psychiatrists run into each other on the street. The first to speak says, *"You're fine. How'm I doing?"*

Patient: You've got to help me, Doctor. My wife thinks she's a pretzel.
Wacky doctor: Bring her in to see me. Maybe I can straighten her out.

Doctor: Ask the accident victim what his name is so we can notify his family.
Nurse: He says his family already knows his name.

Patient: Doctor, if a person's brain stops working, does he die?
Wacky doctor: How can you ask such a stupid question! You're alive, aren't you?

Patient: Doctor, do you think cranberries are healthy?
Wacky doctor: Well, I've never heard one complain.

Nurse: There's a man outside with a wooden leg named Smith.
Wacky doctor: What's the name of his other leg?

Doctor: Deep breathing, you understand,
    destroys germs.
Wacky patient: Yes, Doctor, but how can I
    force them to breathe deeply?

54
Wacky Thoughts

Have you ever seen a ball park?

Have you ever seen a board walk?

Did you ever see the Catskill Mountains?
No, but I've seen them kill mice.

Have you ever seen a fire fly?

Have you ever seen a key punch?

Have you ever seen a king fish?

Have you ever seen a ginger snap?

Have you ever seen a hog bristle?

Have you ever seen a home run?

Have you ever seen a hot dog stand?

Have you ever seen a salad bowl?

Have you ever seen a shoe box?

Have you ever seen a square dance?

Have you ever seen a stone step?

Have you ever seen a tree bark?

Have you ever seen a uniform smile?

55

Wacky Students

I have one teacher who is so forgetful he gave the same test three weeks in a row. If he does that two more times, I may pass it.

First student: My teacher thinks I'm a perfect idiot.
Second student: Well, she's wrong. Nobody's perfect.

Teacher: How long did Thomas Edison live?
Wacky student: All his life.

Teacher: You got a perfect zero on your exam. How did you do it?
Wacky student: It was luck. I guessed at some of the answers.

✦◦✦

Teacher: You can always spot an abnormal student. He's the one who comes back to school from a long vacation and remembers to bring his homework.

✦◦✦

Teacher: Who can tell us something about Good Friday?
Wacky student: He was the fellow who helped Robinson Crusoe

✦◦✦

Teacher: What do you expect to be when you get out of school?
Wacky student: An old man.

✦◦✦

Teacher: Winslow, what's the definition of ignorance?
Winslow: I don't know.

✦◦✦

Teacher: When did Napoleon die?
Wacky student: Die? I didn't even know he was sick.

56
Still More Wacky Definitions

Alarm clock: *A frightened timepiece.*

❧

Applause: *Two hands slapping each other's faces.*

❧

Atoll: *What you pay before you cross a bridge.*

❧

Author: *Someone who's usually write.*

❧

Bedrock: *Any rocks you find in your bed.*

❧

Bully: *A person with more muscles and less brains than anyone else.*

College cheer: *Money from home.*

Comedian: *A person with a good memory who hopes other people don't.*

Finland: *A place where a lot of sharks live.*

Fireproof: *The boss' relatives.*

High Heel: *The invention of a girl who'd been kissed on the forehead one too many times.*

Flabbergasted: *The state you get in when you're overwhelmed by a flabber.*

Hypodermic needle: *A sick-shooter.*

Love: *A heart attack.*

Post Office: *U.S. Snail.*

✂～o～

Sweater: *A garment worn by a small child when his mother feels chilly.*

✂～o～

Thief: *A person who has the habit of finding things before the owner loses them.*

✂～o～

Twins: *Infant replay.*

✂～o～

Work: *An unpopular way of earning money.*

57

Even More Wacky Knock-Knocks

Knock, knock.
Who's there?
Despair.
Despair who?
Despair tire is flat.

❧

Knock, knock.
Who's there?
A herd.
A herd who?
A herd you were home, so I came over!

❧

Knock, knock.
Who's there?
P.
P. who?
P.U.

Knock, knock.
Who's there?
Gillette.
Gillette who?
Gillette the cat out?

Knock, knock.
Who's there?
Celeste.
Celeste who?
Celeste time I'll ask you.

Knock, knock.
Who's there?
Alfred.
Alfred who?
Alfred the needle if you'll sew on the button.

Knock, knock.
Who's there?
Amis.
Amis who?
Amis is as good as a mile.

Knock, knock.
Who's there?

Radio.
Radio who?
Radio not, here I come.

Knock, knock.
Who's there?
Doughnut.
Doughnut who?
Doughnut open until Christmas.

Knock, knock.
Who's there?
Oliver.
Oliver who?
Oliver troubles will soon be over.

Knock, knock.
Who's there?
Yule.
Yule who?
Yule come on down, you hear?

Knock, knock.
Who's there?
Osborn.
Osborn who?
Osborn in the state of Georgia.

Knock, knock.
Who's there?
Pecan.
Pecan who?
Pecan somebody your own size.

Knock, knock.
Who's there?
Polly Warner.
Polly Warner who?
Polly Warner Cracker.

Knock, knock.
Who's there?
Sherwood.
Sherwood who?
Sherwood like you to let me in.

Knock, knock.
Who's there?
Howard.
Howard who?
Howard you today?

Knock, knock.
Who's there?

Phillip.
Phillip who?
Phillip the tub so I can take a bath.

Knock, knock.
Who's there?
Nixon.
Nixon who?
Nixon stones will break my bones.

Knock, knock.
Who's there?
Sarah.
Sarah who?
Sarah doctor in the house?

Knock, knock.
Who's there?
Howie.
Howie who?
Fine, thanks. Howie you?